Coloring and Tracing

Meimei---Let's Count! 美美---让我们数一数!

written and illustrated by Yue Chen

Dedication

I dedicate this book to YOU! Thanks for supporting *MeimeiStory* book series! Hope you enjoy tracing and coloring this book.

4

yī

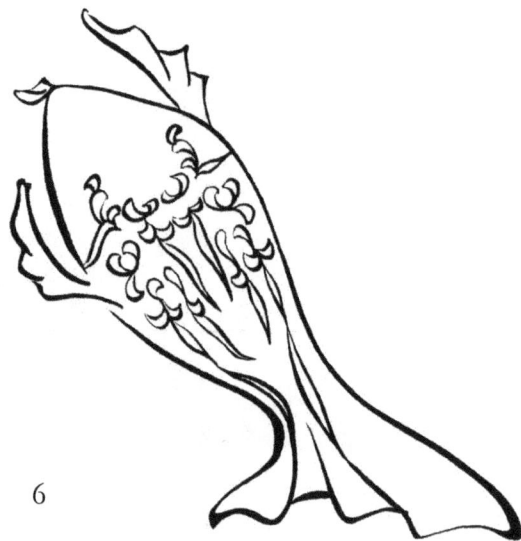

6

èr

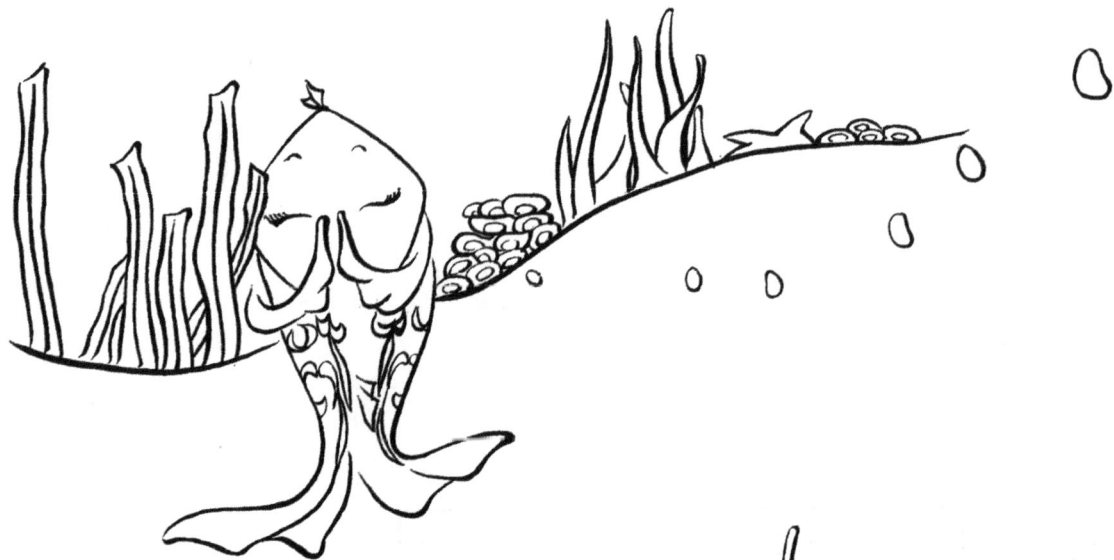

sān

sì

wǔ

liù

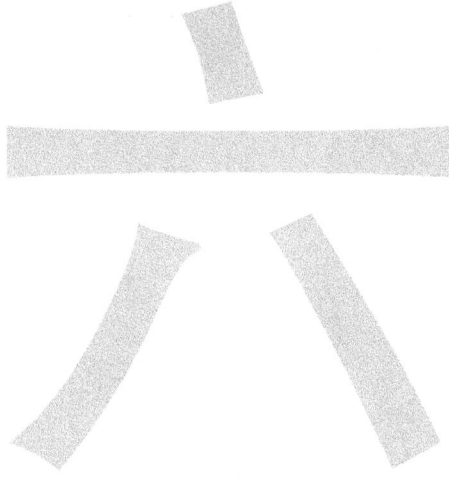

16

bā

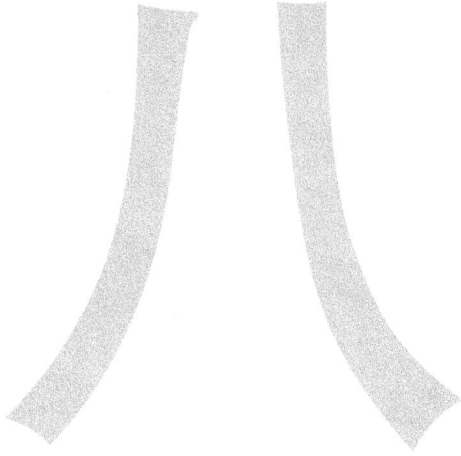

jiǔ

22

shí

Are you ready? Let's Count!

1

2   3

4

yī   èr   sān   sì

一,   二,   三,   四,

5   6   10

8

7

9

wǔ   liù   qī   bā   jiǔ   shí

五，六，七，八，九，十！

一　二　三　四　五　六　七　八　九　十

jiǔ
èr
sì
bā
sān
shí
wǔ
yī
liù
qī

28

Let's match them up!

yī	three
èr	ten
sān	eight
sì	one
wǔ	four
liù	two
qī	seven
bā	six
jiǔ	five
shí	nine

(A line connects "yī" to "one")

29